Folk Festivals

American Folklore

Children's Folklore
Christmas and Santa Claus Folklore
Contemporary Folklore
Ethnic Folklore
Family Folklore
Firefighters' Folklore
Folk Arts and Crafts
Folk Customs
Folk Dance
Folk Fashion
Folk Festivals
Folk Games
Folk Medicine
Folk Music
Folk Proverbs and Riddles
Folk Religion
Folk Songs
Folk Speech
Folk Tales and Legends
Food Folklore
Regional Folklore

North American Folklore

Folk Festivals

by Ellyn Sanna

Mason Crest Publishers

Mason Crest Publishers Inc.
370 Reed Road
Broomall, Pennsylvania 19008
(866) MCP-BOOK (toll free)
www.masoncrest.com

Copyright © 2003 by Mason Crest Publishers. All rights reserved. No part of this publication may be reproduced or transmitted in any form or by any means, electronic or mechanical, including photocopying, recording, taping, or any information storage and retrieval system, without permission from the publisher.

First printing
1 2 3 4 5 6 7 8 9 10
Library of Congress Cataloging-in-Publication Data on file at the Library of Congress.
ISBN 1-59084-340-1
     1-59084-328-2 (series)

Design by Lori Holland.
Page composition by Bytheway Publishing Services, Binghamton, New York.
Cover Design by Joe Gilmore.
Printed and bound in the Hashemite Kingdom of Jordan.

Picture credits:
Cover: "Halloween Scare" by Frederic Stanley. © 1935 SEPS: Licensed by Curtis Publishing, Indianapolis, IN. www.curtispublishing.com

Contents

Introduction   *1*

1. *Circles in Time: Marking Life's Seasons*   *7*
2. *Festivals of Light and Giving: Winter Holidays*   *21*
3. *Signs of New Life: Late Winter Celebrations*   *37*
4. *Resurrection Celebrations: Spring Rites*   *45*
5. *Those Lazy, Hazy Days of Summer: Celebrations of Love and Freedom*   *59*
6. *Glimpses of Another World: Halloween and Other Celebrations of the Supernatural*   *67*
7. *Harvest Home: Feasts of Gratitude*   *77*
8. *A Three-Strand Spiral: Celebrating the Past, the Community, and the Spiritual World*   *89*

Further Reading   *102*
For More Information   *103*
Glossary   *104*
Index   *105*

Folklore grows from long-ago seeds. Just as an acorn sends down roots even as it shoots up leaves across the sky, folklore is rooted deeply in the past and yet still lives and grows today. It spreads through our modern world with branches as wide and sturdy as any oak's; it grounds us in yesterday even as it helps us make sense of both the present and the future.

Introduction

by Dr. Alan Jabbour

WHAT do a tale, a joke, a fiddle tune, a quilt, a jig, a game of jacks, a saint's day procession, a snake fence, and a Halloween costume have in common? Not much, at first glance, but all these forms of human creativity are part of a zone of our cultural life and experience that we sometimes call "folklore."

The word "folklore" means the cultural traditions that are learned and passed along by ordinary people as part of the fabric of their lives and culture. Folklore may be passed along in verbal form, like the urban legend that we hear about from friends who assure us that it really happened to a friend of their cousin. Or it may be tunes or dance steps we pick up on the block, or ways of shaping things to use or admire out of materials readily available to us, like that quilt our aunt made. Often we acquire folklore without even fully realizing where or how we learned it.

Though we might imagine that the word "folklore" refers to cultural traditions from far away or long ago, we actually use and enjoy folklore as part of our own daily lives. It is often ordinary, yet we often remember and prize it because it seems somehow very special. Folklore is culture we share with others in our communities, and we build our identities through the sharing. Our first shared identity is family identity, and family folklore such as shared meals or prayers or songs helps us develop a sense of belonging. But as we grow older we learn to belong to other groups as well. Our identities may be ethnic, religious, occupational, or regional—or all of these, since no one has only one cultural identity. But in every case the identity is anchored and strengthened by a variety of cultural traditions we participate in and share with our neighbors. We feel the threads of connection with people we know, but the threads extend far beyond our own immediate communities. In a real sense they connect us in one way or another to the world.

Folklore possesses features by which we distinguish ourselves from each other. A certain dance step may be African American, or a certain story urban, or a certain hymn Protestant, or a certain food preparation Cajun. Folklore can distinguish us, but at the same time it is one of the best ways we introduce ourselves to each other. We learn about new ethnic groups on the North American landscape by sampling their cuisine, and we enthusiastically adopt musical ideas from other communities. Stories, songs, and visual designs move from group to group, enriching all people in the process. Folklore thus is both a sign of identity, experienced as a special marker of our special groups, and at the same time a cultural coin that is well spent by sharing with others beyond our group boundaries.

Folklore is usually learned informally. Somebody, somewhere, taught us that jump rope rhyme we know, but we may have trouble remembering just where we got it, and it probably wasn't in a book that was assigned as homework. Our world has a domain of formal knowledge, but folklore is a domain of knowledge and culture that is learned by sharing and imitation rather than formal instruction. We can study it formally—that's what we are doing now!—but its natural arena is in the informal, person-to-person fabric of our lives.

Not all culture is folklore. Classical music, art sculpture, or great novels are forms of high art that may contain folklore but are not themselves folklore. Popular music or art may be built on folklore themes and traditions, but it addresses a much wider and more diverse audience than folk music or folk art. But even in the world of popular and mass culture, folklore keeps popping

Introduction

up around the margins. E-mail is not folklore—but an e-mail smile is. And college football is not folklore—but the wave we do at the stadium is.

This series of volumes explores the many faces of folklore throughout the North American continent. By illuminating the many aspects of folklore in our lives, we hope to help readers of the series to appreciate more fully the richness of the cultural fabric they either possess already or can easily encounter as they interact with their North American neighbors.

Some people use the seasons of their faith as a "map" for keeping track of time.

ONE

Circles in Time
Marking Life's Seasons

Children are not born with a concept of time. From their parents and teachers they learn to measure time and shape it into patterns.

WHEN MY SON was very young, he was given a set of colorful magnets that included the days of the week. Each morning Gabe would ask me the name of the new day. Sunday happened to be the first day he began this activity, and so I fished around in his bag of magnets and found the word Sunday. Gabe put it on the refrigerator with a satisfied air that the day had been properly named.

The following morning he did the same thing, and then again the next day, until at last we had a long straggling line of words stretching across the refrigerator door: Sunday, Monday, Tuesday, Wednesday, Thursday, Friday, Saturday. On the eighth day, instead of handing him a new magnet for his long line of days, I pointed back to Sunday.

My son scowled, puzzled by my insistence that we start all over again. He had only just grasped the concept that each day was a separate space of time with an identity all its own. Now, in his mind, I might as well have given birth to a new child and insisted we use the name Gabe over again. He may have thought I had simply run out of ideas for names; I'm sure together we could have come up with some alternatives that would have made just as much sense to him as the seven I had already named—Purpleday, for instance, or Kittyday would probably have been his favorites.

Gabe and I sat together on the floor, staring at the refrigerator, both of us thinking. After a moment, I had an idea. I shifted the long line of magnets into a circle.

Gabe studied the new arrangement for a moment. Then he

nodded. "Days don't go in lines," he said, with an expression that indicated, Why didn't you say so before? "Days go in circles."

DAYS—and months and years, as well—do go in circles. Today, we often think of time as a long line stretching endlessly into the future—but our oldest traditions remind us that, at least in some sense, time is a circle. Today it may be Monday, the beginning of the school week, but the weekend will come, just as it always does, a never-ending pattern of work and rest, studies and free time. Even better, summer vacation will come again . . . and the Christmas holidays . . . and your birthday. Like a wheel that never stops turning, time's circle goes round and round.

We measure where we are on the circle by naming and numbering the days and months and years. As we keep track of our place in time, holidays also give us a "language" to mark the circle. "The concert is after Christmas," we say. Or, "By Easter time, I will have reached my goal." We also use holidays as markers for the past: "I haven't seen you since the Fourth of July picnic." Or, "You were born right before Thanksgiving."

We all have our own mental maps of time, with important days standing out like lines on a measuring stick. For instance, for most students the first and last days of school are the markers that give shape to the year's circle of days. For a business person, the fiscal year may be the cycle that's most important to them, and

> Will the circle be unbroken,
> By and by, Lord, by and by?
> —*religious folksong*

Native Americans' connection to the earth was intimate and vital. The earth's events were the high points of their lives. Today's Iroquois people still celebrate each of these:

- the maple ceremony (when the sap begins to run);
- the planting ceremony;
- the green corn ceremony;
- the strawberry festival;
- the green bean festival;
- the harvest festival; and
- the midwinter festival (when the Pleiades are directly overhead).

Today we may think of fall as a cozy and colorful time. But early cultures feared autumn's shorter, colder days, since the trees' bright leaves signaled the coming of winter.

> *Many cultures link time, the earth's seasons, and the will of God, as this African American folktale illustrates:*
>
> A slaveowner planted a crop of corn—but just as it got up pretty good, along came a drought and dried up his corn. So he prayed for rain. He prayed, and everyone prayed, and then he prayed some more.
>
> But no rain came, and his corn died in the field. Just when it was as dry and yellow as it could be, past any hope of life, a big gray cloud came across the sky. The man was furious. He called to his slaves and made them pull up all the corn. "If God wouldn't rain on my corn when it needed it," he muttered, "I won't let Him rain on it now."
>
> The rain began to fall just as the corn was all pulled up. Cursing, the man went into his house. He heard a whirring noise and looked up at his mantle, where an empty clock case stood—and he was thunderstruck to hear that empty case strike twelve. The man was furious with God. He ran back outside to shake his fist at the sky—and the lightning shot down and killed him dead. I guess God answered him all right.
>
> Adapted from *Storytellers: Folktales and Legends from the South*, edited by John A. Burrison (Athens: University of Georgia Press, 1993), p. 299.

April 15th, the day when income taxes are due, may be the year's most prominent marker. Other people may rely on the religious year, with its cycle of holy days and seasons, to measure their concept of time. Some people may use sports for their mental map for time, enjoying the yearly round of baseball, swimming, and golf—and then on to football, basketball, and skiing. For many of us, one or more of these mental maps coexist in our heads at the same time.

These "time maps" are taught to us by our parents, our schools, our culture. But like young children, long-ago early societies lacked these patterns to make sense out of the passage of time. They noticed the changing cycles of light and dark, warmth and cold, of course, but they found this phenomenon mysterious and even frightening. Each time the sun departed, they wondered if it would return. Every time the earth grew cold and died, they feared that warmth and life would not return. These early cultures told themselves stories to explain these circles in time.

For instance, an ancient Mexican folktale says that at the very beginning of the world, time and space were created in the same instance. During these first moments of creation, the Creator Parents gave birth to two sons, Tezcatlipoca and Quetzalcoatl. These two each wanted to carry the sun—and they fought each other fiercely for the honor. During their battles, they knocked the sun from the sky, bringing cold and destruction to the earth.

At last Tezcatlipoca and Quetzalcoatl realized that they must stop their fighting or the earth would not survive. The sky had fallen to the earth, and nothing could live amid such devastation. So the brothers planted themselves one on each end of the fallen sky, and they became towering trees that would grow forever. They lifted the fallen sky between them, and then they walked across it and met in the middle. As they walked, they scattered sparks of light, and their path became the Milky Way.

But still the sun would not rise in the sky, for it was too broken. One of the divine beings, a poor and humble god named Nanahuatzin, offered to give his life to save the sun. He leapt into its fires—and he was transformed into the sun. Out of his sacrifice, the sun was reborn and rose again.

The other gods gave Huitzilpochtli, the god of war, the job of

Ancient Mexicans used carvings like this to express their belief that time was a circle.

carrying the sun on his back across the sky. Each dawn, Huitzilpochtli battles the darkness. Each day, he wins for a time, and the sun rises in the sky. Although night reclaims the earth, Huitzilpochtli never gives up fighting back the darkness. In winter, Huitzilpochtli grows weak, and the sun does not rise as high—and people must help him by their acts of sacrifice. Because of his courage and strength, however, the people of the earth can sleep secure at night, knowing light will always return to the earth.

Circles in Time

STORIES like these helped early cultures make sense of their world. Today, our oldest folk traditions still use the Earth's cycles of death and renewal to map time. Our ancestors lived far more closely to the Earth than most of us do today, and they were intimately aware of its patterns: seeds grew in the spring;

Rituals are a vital element of all folk festivals. These rituals are repeated patterns of action. They may be as obvious and important as going to church on Easter—or as seemingly small and inconsequential as barbequing hotdogs on the Fourth of July.

Rituals are like **metaphors** in action that carry with them a deeper meaning. For instance, lighting a candle may symbolize the community's belief in eternal life—and reenacting the details of past events (as Jews do when they eat the bitter herb at Passover or Christians do when they make a manger for Baby Jesus at Christmas) reminds people of their central beliefs about life's meaning.

Repeating these rituals over and over, the same way each year, is one reason why holidays often seem as though they are little spaces outside linear time. They are also what give holidays their unique and distinctive "feel." Holidays just wouldn't be the same without these rituals. That's why, no matter how old you get, you may insist on hanging up your stocking on Christmas Eve. And if you grew up in a northern, colder climate but end up moving to the South as an adult, you may find yourself turning up the air-conditioning, building a fire, and sipping hot chocolate to celebrate Christmas.

plants matured in the summer; harvest came in the fall; dormancy and death came in the winter. New light and new warmth meant death would not win, and people were filled with relief and joy each time life returned to the earth. Most folk celebrations were connected in some way to the earth's ever-revolving circle.

Hundreds of years ago, people had no way to measure time. The

Folktales seek to explain the earth's seasons and the passage of time.

Western civilization has become obsessed with numbers. We count and measure everything—and by doing so, we change the way we think about things. Almost always, we connect value judgments to our measurements. As a teenager, you know that your age number implies certain things to the rest of the world; you're no longer a child but not yet quite an adult. Twenty-one has become the magic number that means full adulthood. As you get older, however, your age number carries a different value; past 30, and age becomes an embarrassment, something of which we may be ashamed. But the concept of time in folk traditions is very different; in fact, some cultures, like the Algonquin Indians, don't even have a word for time.

Today, our concept of time may be unhealthy. We speak of being "pressed for time," "short on time," "out of time." Researchers wonder if the way we think about time has become one factor in the prevalence of heart disease and other stress-related illnesses.

Many North Americans fear the passage of time—but folk festivals celebrate time's passage. From this perspective, time is a reason for joy. Time gives us good gifts. Its circle is wide and rich and bountiful.

earth itself and the moon were their only clocks. Early cultures used these natural cycles to impose a pattern on their lives, a pattern that would help them make sense out of their experiences. Festivals and holidays were one way they gave meaning to their existence.

The word "festival" is rooted in two Latin words (festum and feria); one means "public joy and merriment," while the other implied a time free from work in order to honor the gods. The root meaning of "holiday" may be more obvious: holy-day was the original spelling of this word. When we look at the long-ago roots for these familiar words, we can understand better the importance of festivals and holidays in folk traditions. These were

A birthday is a festival shared by a small community of friends and family.

Birthdays are private, personal festivals. Like many festivals, food plays a central part in the celebration; what would a birthday be without a cake? When your family and friends gather around to sing "Happy Birthday," they are acting out an important ritual. The candles mark your procession through life, another tiny light for each year of your life. The community's love and attention is all focused on you, just as it was on the day of your birth. You blow out your candles, demonstrating the power of your life (your breath), your control over the past, and your wish for the future—and then everyone has a piece of cake. You probably take this small, ordinary ritual for granted, but like many religious holiday rituals, it contains the important elements of light, song, and shared food.

special, social days, days when the entire community gathered together to have fun—and these days were also sacred, for they linked the community with something deeper, something that gave them a sense of connection to the spiritual world.

Today we still see holidays and festivals as occasions for good times and togetherness—and we also see them as opportunities to celebrate life's deepest meanings. Each of our important holidays remains deeply rooted in folk traditions. Although we may have forgotten the reasons why we celebrate when we do, these special days still link us to the earth's ancient cycle.

In the midst of winter's cold and snow, folk traditions like the Christmas tree affirm life's power. Rituals of both light and giving will be enacted around each family's tree.

TWO

Festivals of Light and Giving
Winter Holidays

Folktales often create human personalities for winter and other seasons.

ONCE LONG AGO, a selfish widow lived with her daughter and stepdaughter. The woman's daughter was as self-centered as she was, but her stepdaughter was a kind and thoughtful girl. The woman and her daughter hated the stepdaughter, however, and they made her do all their work, including the spinning.

The girl spun so much that her fingers bled. One day, as she was leaning over the well to rinse the blood from her fingers, her spindle slipped out of her fingers and dropped into the water. "You stupid, clumsy thing!" her stepmother shrieked. "Don't just sit there! Get down in that well and find the spindle." She gave the poor girl a push—and down the stepdaughter tumbled, deeper and deeper into the well.

When she opened her eyes, expecting to find herself drowning, she saw instead that she was in a strange and lovely world she had never seen before. She got to her feet and began to walk, looking around her.

She came to a baker's oven beside the path, where bread was baking. To her surprise, a voice called from the oven, "Quick! Take us out please. We're about to burn."

The girl opened the oven and took out the bread, and then she continued on her way.

She came next to an apple tree that was heavy with fruit. "Shake me!" the tree cried. "My fruit is ripe and needs to fall."

The girl obligingly shook the tree until the apples tumbled onto the ground, and then she went on her way. This time she came to a tiny house where an old woman stood in the doorway.

"Oh, child, won't you come and help me?" the old woman squeaked. "I have so much work to do."

The girl couldn't help but notice that the old woman had enormous teeth. Gathering her courage, though, she agreed to help, and the old woman led her into the tiny house.  An immense feather bed lay on the floor. They each took a corner and dragged it outdoors, where they shook it until the feathers flew through the air.

The old woman laughed and clapped her hands. "It's snowing, it's snowing! I am Mother Holle, and you have helped me make it snow."

The old woman fed the girl a rich and tasty meal. "Now I will lead you back to your own world." She took the girl's hand and led her through the thick snow, to a door that led back into her own world. "Thank you for having a generous heart," the old woman said. "You shall have everything you need."

As the girl stepped through the doorway, she found the lost spindle in her hand. Even better, in the midst of the snow a shower of gold fell over her and clung to her hair and clothes.

Her stepmother and her stepsister were amazed when they say her. Immediately, her stepsister decided she would go find Mother Holle, so that she too could be covered with gold. She dove down the well and started walking. "Help me!" cried a loaf of bread from the oven by her path. "I'm burning!"

"Too bad!" snarled the stepsister.

"Shake me!" called an apple tree. "Oh please free me from this burden of ripe apples."

But the stepsister just kept walking. "They will fall by themselves soon enough," she called impatiently over shoulder.

When she reached the house of Mother Holle at last, the old woman was once more struggling with her feather mattress. But it looked too heavy to the stepsister.

"If the bed is not shaken, the snow will not fall," the old woman explained.

"Who needs snow anyway?" the girl said, tossing her head.

She was so lazy that Mother Holle soon sent her on her way, back to her own world. The girl eagerly plunged through the door, expecting a shower of gold.

Instead, toads tumbled over her head. She ran home crying, toads hopping from her skirts all the way.

> The first historical reference to a December celebration of Christ's birth was in A.D. 336. It was first called Christ Mass in 1038, and the words eventually evolved into Christmas.

GERMAN SETTLERS brought this folktale to the New World, but for thousands of years before that, folklore had linked winter with generosity. Mother Holle's winter snows might be beautiful, but they also brought the "starving time," a time of cold and food shortages. Those who opened their hearts and hands

In the 19th century, the Christmas tree became an enduring part of North American Christmas traditions.

to others during this time were blessed—and those who refused to share what they had were the poorer for their greediness.

Many folk celebrations are connected to December 21, the winter *solstice*, the day with the shortest number of daylight hours in all the year. Ancient cultures began the tradition of celebration. The Babylonians had a winter festi-

The Orthodox Church still follows the old Julian calendar, rather than the "new" one introduced by Pope Gregory in 1582. According to the Julian calendar, Christmas falls on January 7.

Festivals of Light and Giving

val called Zagmuk, and the Persians celebrated the birth of the god Mithra, the Unconquerable Sun, on December 25. The long-ago Romans continued the tradition with their Saturnalia celebrations. During Saturnalia, trees were decorated with candles and gifts were exchanged.

As Christianity spread throughout the world, it gave new meaning to this holiday and its traditions. Christians began to celebrate Christ's **nativity** on December 25th, and they adopted many of the older customs as symbols of Christ's birth. Christmas became a festival of light and gifts, expressing the birth of divine Light and Love into the world.

Different cultures, however, had different traditions to express these same themes. The Norse burned the Yule log, sym-

North Americans' image of Santa Claus has evolved over the years. In the 19th century, he was often imagined riding a horse (rather than driving a sleigh pulled by reindeer).

bolizing a light that never dies. The Celts decorated their homes with evergreen and holly, affirming life's endless victory. The Irish, British, and Scandinavian descendents of these people brought their traditions with them to North America. So did Dutch settlers, who told the story of kind Saint Nicholas (or Sinterklaas) and his companion Black Piet. These two climbed up onto the rooftops and dropped gifts and candy down the chimneys, where they fell into children's stockings and wooden shoes.

Some settlers in the New World, like the Dutch, honored their Christmas traditions on December 5; others, like the Greeks, celebrated the holiday early in January. Gradually, however, December 25th became North America's most important holiday. Folk traditions still varied from region to region, of course. For instance, in Newfoundland, many children dress up in costumes and go from door to door for food and drink, while Mexi-

---

New Year's Day and Christmas have traditionally been linked together. During the 19th century, North Americans often exchanged gifts on New Year's Day rather than on Christmas, and New Year's cards of the 19th century were typically decorated with pictures of holly and candles, images we today connect with Christmas. In Old Dutch New York, Santa traditionally came on January 1st.

For Polish Americans, *wigilia* is a part of their Christmas celebrations. This meatless meal began on Christmas Eve, as soon as the first star was sighted in the sky. (Children stayed out of their busy mothers' way, searching the sky for that first spark of light.) An empty place was always set at the table; according to some traditions, this place was for Christ, but other families considered it to be a place for a recently deceased family member or for an unexpected guest. Straw or hay would be placed under the tablecloth to remind the family of Christ's manger, and a **communion**-like wafer would be a central part of the meal.

Festivals of Light and Giving

can Americans make tamales by the hundreds in honor of the festival. People in Alaska go "starring," holding a twirling star above their heads while they sing carols; and Moravians light the Christingle, an orange decorated with fruit and a candle to represent the light of Christ. But whether they pray and fast, or feast and dance, nearly all cultures celebrate Christmas with light and gifts.

Not everyone living in North America is a Christian, however. Children growing up in these other religious traditions could not help but look wistfully at the Christmas extravaganza of bright lights and heaped packages. Jewish Americans decided to create their own alternative to Christmas. They chose a holy day that until then had never been a particularly important one within the Jewish calendar—Hanukkah, the festival of lights.

Hanukkah (or Chanukah) starts on the 25th day of the Jewish

At Hanukkah children enjoy spinning dreidels. When playing the game, the Hebrew letters on each side of the dreidel stand for nun (nothing), gimmel (get all), hey (get half), and shin (shove in).

Children play an important role in holiday traditions.

month of Kislev (which is usually in December). The festival celebrates the defeat of the Greeks by Judas Maccabaeus and his followers nearly 2,000 years ago. After his victory, the Jewish people worked to clean up their temple in Jerusalem. When everything was in order once more, they celebrated. As part of their festival, they lit the temple's special lamp—only to find they had only enough oil to last one night. A messenger was sent for more oil, but the people knew it would take him four days to return. Still, they lit the lamp and went ahead with their celebration, singing and playing cymbals and harps in God's praise. Day

Festivals of Light and Giving 31

after day, night after night, the flame in the special lamp kept burning. When the messenger returned eight days later, it was still lit.

In North America today, Jews continue to celebrate this miracle with the menorah (a branched candlestick holding eight or nine candles). On each day of Hanukkah, they light a new candle and give small gifts to the children in the family.

In 1966, a man from yet another ethnic background felt the

Some people may find today's Christmas traditions to be garish and overdone. But this house decorated with hundreds of electric lights is a modern celebration of light and life in the midst of winter's dark and cold.

The lights on the Christmas tree symbolize many things—warmth, family, love, heritage, togetherness, and enduring life.

Festivals of Light and Giving

> The candles in Kwanzaa's seven-branched candelabra stand for:
>
> - unity;
> - self-determination;
> - collective work and responsibility;
> - cooperative economics;
> - purpose;
> - creativity; and
> - faith.

need to affirm his own cultural identity in the midst of North America's Christmas celebrations. Dr. Maulana (Ron) Kurenga was a Nigerian teaching at a university in California. He decided to use the light traditions found in Christmas and Hanukkah celebrations and combine them with African harvest celebrations. He created the holiday of Kwanzaa, celebrated for seven days beginning on December 26th. It was not meant to be an alternative to either Christmas or Hanukkah, but rather an affirmation of African Americans' cultural identity.

Kwanzaa is a new celebration, and some say it was created artificially, rather than being a natural outgrowth from a body of folk traditions. However, since its beginning in the 1960s, the holiday has spread through the African American community; by 1992, over 18 million North Americans observed Kwanzaa. Perhaps it caught on so quickly because it was deeply rooted in ancient traditions.

Other cultures also celebrate winter festivals of giving. For instance, the Native Americans of the Northwest hold "potlatches." These festivals do not always occur at the same time; instead, the chief can call a potlatch at any time of community stress. In one case, during the two-week ceremony the chief fed several hundred guests. He gave to his guests 18,000 blankets, 700 silver bracelets, a dozen canoes, sewing machines, pots and pans, hundreds of sacks of flour, sugar, fruit, and cash. These acts of generosity spring from the tribe's belief that the Great Spirit created the world as a gift to humanity—and when humans give gifts to one another, they echo the divine act of creation and put themselves in harmony with the essential nature

Kwanzaa is a new holiday that has quickly caught on in North America. Like Christmas and Hanukkah, it celebrates light and life; it also affirms African American identity.

of the universe. Gift-giving is a symbolic re-creation of the universe—and it strengthens the community by creating the bonds necessary for the group's healthy functioning.

North America's Christmas traditions may sometimes seem to have lost this sense of meaning. It lies hidden beneath the rush of shopping days and the glare of garish decorations . . . but at the heart of Christmas still lies a deep-rooted folk tradition of giving and light. Christmas, like all winter festivals, celebrates light in the midst of darkness. It affirms that life lives on even in the midst of winter—and as we give to one another, new beginnings spring out of the coldest, darkest night.

Valentine's Day traditions offer color and excitement as winter is growing old.

THREE

Signs of New Life
Late Winter Celebrations

Birds were a common image on early valentines.

By MID-FEBRUARY, we're usually tired of winter. Christmas is long ago; spring is still too far away. We need something to give us hope.

VALENTINE'S DAY

IN THE MIDST of February, the ancient Romans celebrated Lupercalia, in honor of the mother wolf who was said to have cared for Romulus and Remus, the mythical twin founders of Rome. The holiday was celebrated with partying and dancing. Some people dipped themselves in blood, dying themselves red. Couples paired up, and everybody had a good time.

They had such a good time, in fact, that Christian priests were eager to calm down the celebration. In A.D. 469, the holy day of Saint Valentine was instituted.

The real St. Valentine, if he existed, is lost in the fogs of history. There may in fact have been several historical Valentines. One was a priest who continued to perform secret marriages after the Roman emperor Claudius II had forbidden them. (Young men with wives were less eager to serve in the army—and Claudius had military ambitions that depended on plenty of recruits.) This particular Valentine was imprisoned for disobeying the emperor's edict, and in A.D. 269 he was beheaded. According to one story, while he was in prison, he wrote notes of love to the jailor's daughter; he signed them "Your Valentine."

Valentine's Day is seven weeks after the winter solstice; Halloween is seven weeks before. While Halloween is celebrated with tricks and thoughts of death, Valentine's Day is marked by lace and sentiment and thoughts of love. In a way, they are each other's mirror image.

Nineteenth-century cupids were plump and babyish.

> One of the first valentines was sent by Charles, Duke of Orleans, to his wife in 1415. In 1667, Samuel Pepys speaks in his diary of giving his wife a valentine with gold letters on blue paper.

According to a **medieval** folk tradition, birds chose their mates on February 14th. Lovebirds became a common image that was associated with Valentine's Day. Cupid, the Roman god of love, was also connected to this holiday, and red, the color of blood and hearts, was the day's color.

In the New World, this day for lovers soon became a child's holiday. The powerful god of love, who had once been a strong and dangerous symbol for passion and fertility, was tamed down until he became a mere baby, chubby and harmless. In one-room schoolhouses, children made frilly hearts and slipped them into each other's Valentine boxes.

Today, greeting card companies—as well as candy manufacturers, florists, and jewelers—have taken advantage of an ancient folk holiday as a time to sell their products. Their efforts help to keep this ancient tradition alive and well. Lovers exchange gifts, and school children still slip bright red hearts into each other's Valentine boxes.

GROUNDHOG'S DAY

GROUNDHOG'S DAY is another North American holiday that holds out the promise of spring. If the woodchuck who lives

The companies that sell flowers and candy do good business on Valentine's Day.

Signs of New Life

> The Iroquois people celebrated a midwinter festival that included an ashes-stirring ceremony. Old fires were used to kindle new ones, symbolizing the renewal of dreams and life.

in Punxsutawney, Pennsylvania, sees his shadow on February 2, then we will have six more weeks of winter. If he doesn't, however, an early spring is on its way.

Polish settlers to the New World also celebrated Candlemas Day on February 2nd. On that day, they brought their candles to church to be blessed by the priest. These candles were then thought to protect a house from lightning and thunder; 19th-century prayer books contained special prayers to say during thunderstorms.

According to a Polish proverb, "If there's frost on Candlemas, prepare the wagon; if rain, the sleigh." Rather than watching for a groundhog, these settlers kept their eyes on bears. If a bear came out of his den and found frost, he would tear his den apart because he wouldn't be needing it—but if the day were damp instead, he would mend his den and get it ready for another six weeks of winter weather.

MIDWINTER HOLIDAYS carry the promise that new life lies ahead. The days are growing longer; the earth is stirring with new life. And so are we.

Rabbits and flowers are traditional symbols of spring's new life and fertility.

FOUR

Resurrection Celebrations
Spring Rites

Like many other cultures, Native Americans of the Northeast pictured the seasons as powerful human beings.

O NCE LONG AGO, when the world was new, an old man with long, white hair wandered across the earth. Wherever he stepped, the soil turned hard as stone, and whenever he breathed, the rivers stood still and frozen, and the lakes turned to ice. Plants turned black and shriveled, and animals fled before him. The old man built himself a lodge of ice and snow, and he settled down, knowing that his home was built to last forever.

But one day he heard a knocking at his door. Whoever was outside banged so hard that chunks of ice from the walls cracked and fell onto the ground. But the old man only sneered and hunched his shoulders. "Go away!" he shouted. "No one can come in my—"

But before he could finish his sentence, the door of his lodge broke in two and fell to the ground. A smiling young man stepped inside, holding a green stick. He stirred the old man's cold fire until it leaped high and hot.

The old man began to sweat. "Who are you?" he cried. "I want you to leave. Be gone with you, or I will freeze you with my breath!"

The young man only laughed. "Old Man, you cannot frighten me. Don't you know who I am? Wherever I step, the snow melts and grass grows. Whenever I breathe, flowers bloom and the animals grow big with new life. It is your time to leave."

The old man tried to freeze the young man with his breath—but only a thin cool mist came from the old man's thin blue lips. Sweat poured from his brow, and he grew smaller and smaller. At last he melted away, and the ice walls of his lodge fell to the ground in slushy piles. Soon, white flowers grew instead of snow.

Once again, Spring had conquered Winter.

THE Seneca people of the Northeast Woodlands told this folktale to explain spring's new life. The ***immigrants*** from other nations around the world brought their own spring stories to North America. These folk stories reflect very different cultures, religions, and traditions—but all, in one way or another, describe spring's resurrection from the dead.

For instance, immigrants from India brought with them the story of Prahlad, the son of King Hiranyakashup. The king wanted his people to worship him, but his own son refused, insisting that he would worship only God (or Vishnu). Furious, the king ordered his son thrown into a pit of poisonous snakes—but the young prince miraculously survived. Next, the king ordered that a herd of elephants be stampeded so they would trample the prince as he slept—but again God protected Prahlad, and he escaped unharmed. Finally, the king asked his wicked sister Holika to destroy his son. Holika was known to be protected from fire, so she took Prahlad to the top of a huge bonfire. The flames danced around them—but God protected Prahlad once again. The prince stepped from the flames unsinged, but Holika was

Folk traditions from India stressed life's power to emerge untouched from the fires of death.

consumed by the flames. Heavenly goodness won over earthly evil.

North Americans of Indian descent still celebrate this tradition at Holi, their festival of spring. They build bonfires and roast nuts. On the next day is the Festival of Color, when they throw buckets of colored water at each other, reflecting the tradition that the gods Krishna and Radha splashed each other in the river when they were enjoying the spring weather. People wear their old clothes and feast, celebrating the victory of good over evil.

Christian traditions rejoice in this same victory by commemorating the death and resurrection of Jesus at Easter time. This is the only festival celebrated in the Christian Church that moves around a bit in the calendar; a deeply religious holiday, it is nevertheless tied to earth and moon, for it follows the first full moon after the spring **equinox** on March 21.

In some regions, the Easter celebration begins with Mardi Gras (or Fat Tuesday), a time of **carnival**, feasting, and dancing.

Traditional Japanese folk customs celebrate spring with bonfires.

Immigrants from northern Europe celebrated this season with tobogganing and feasts. The Finnish Americans in Northern Minnesota still hold "Laskiainen" festivals, where they elect a queen, have sports competitions, and eat plenty of food. The French Canadians who settled Louisiana, had their own Mardi Gras traditions. Theirs involved costumes, dancing, and street parades.

Today, Mardi Gras is a big event in New Orleans and other

Resurrection Celebrations

> Many festivals contain "rites of reversal." This means that people behave the opposite from what they would ordinarily. At Holi, people wear their oldest clothes and drench each other with water; at Mardi Gras, participants do outrageous things in public. These reversals in behavior add to the sense of freedom. They express a wild, rowdy life that is too stubborn to yield to the restraints of winter and death.

communities in Louisiana. It is a time when all the rules are removed, and people can do almost anything. Elaborate floats and costumed spectators parade through the streets. Anything can be thrown into the crowd: beads, coins, even underwear. (After 1986, however, people were no longer allowed to throw coconuts, since getting hit in the head with something hard did not add to anyone's enjoyment.)

After Mardi Gras, comes the Christian season of Lent, the long and solemn stretch of time until Easter, a time when Christians examine their lives while they identify themselves with Christ's self-sacrifice on the cross. Although these 40 days are a deeply spiritual period, the word "Lent" ties the time back to the earth's cycle, for the original Old English word meant simply

At Mardi Gras carnivals, many people wear elaborate masks and costumes.

Resurrection Celebrations

> According to a Welsh folk tradition, the Easter rabbit was a hare, a noble animal who lived alone and hurt no one. He was a Christ-image, for he was willing to sacrifice himself for a fellow hare being chased by a dog or a fox.

"lengthening of days." Easter, Lent's culmination, celebrates Christ's resurrection from the dead—but the word itself also ties this religious celebration back to the earth, for Eostre was the Anglo Saxon word for the goddess of spring.

Some North American Christian traditions have sought to erase the connections between

Decorated eggs are traditional Easter symbols.

A baby chick hatching from its shell is a metaphor for new life triumphing over death.

Christian holy days and the old "***pagan***" earth festivals. Both Catholic and Protestant religious traditions have feared that the older religions would somehow diminish or negate the meaning of Christianity. Other Christian traditions, however—for instance Celtic Christians—welcomed the parallels between Christianity and the ancient celebrations of the earth's cycles. From this perspective, the symbolism of the earth's cycles only deepened the meaning of Christ's life and death—and vice versa.

At Easter, North American folk traditions focus on symbols of new and fertile life—bunnies, lambs, eggs. The egg plays a prominent role in almost all Easter celebrations. Children search for hidden candy eggs; they dye eggs with pastel colors; they eagerly await the chocolate eggs and egg-shaped jelly beans that will fill their Easter baskets. Few of those children will give the egg's meaning a second thought—but the egg is a powerful symbol of resurrection, for it hides new life inside something that ap-

> Some Polish Americans combine both Christian and pagan customs in their Easter celebrations. At the "drowning of Marzanna" a figure representing Death is braided from sheaves of grain into a human form; the ***effigy*** is then immersed in a river or lake, to ensure that Death will not visit the community that year. Later, during Holy Week (the final week of Lent), the same community might erect a grave for Christ. They would bring tulips and daffodils to the grave, and kneel and pray, as though they were attending a ***wake***.

pears to be hard and stone-like. When the baby bird breaks through its shell, it is a resurrection image.

Other religions have their own spring festivals. Jews around the world celebrate Passover, the celebration of the ancient Hebrews' escape from Egypt into freedom. During the spring, Asian Americans celebrate their New Year's with the arrival of the Spring Moon. According to their traditions, April's new life and light represent prosperity and brightness for the coming year.

North Americans from Southeast Asian spend the last day of the old year preparing for the new year. They clean their houses, a traditional custom that's thought to drive away any evil spirits and disasters left from the past. Then comes a day between the old and the new, a time when all work is forbidden and people rest.

On New Year's Day, Laotian Americans tie bright cotton strings around the wrists of friends and loved ones for good luck. Cambodian Americans perform the "wishing dance," where dancers wish prosperity for everyone present. Vietnamese Americans wear new clothes for three days to demonstrate their re-

Many cultures wear new clothes for their spring holiday to symbolize that they are putting on fresh life.

April Fool's Day, the first of April, is another special day in spring. It is thought to have been born out of the confusion that arose in the 16th century when people switched from the old Julian calendar to the new Gregorian one. According to the story, the old calendar had so many flaws that New Year's and Easter ended up coinciding—a foolish thing, according to most people. When Charles IX of France first adopted the new calendar, however, some people refused to change. Others said they were April fools and sent them mock gifts on April 1.

Today there are many April Fool's traditions. Mexican Americans say that if you borrow something on April 1, you don't have to give it back; instead, you send a box of candy with the message "April Fools!" American Hindus celebrate Holi at this same time of year, and they also play practical jokes and send people on foolish errands as part of their celebration.

newal and regeneration. They eat watermelon seeds as a symbol of fertility and life.

North Americans enjoy a rich variety of spring folk traditions and holidays. These festivals may be rooted in faraway lands and in various religious faiths, but they all have something in common. They all celebrate the promise of new life, a promise the earth holds out to us all each year at spring.

Special picnic foods are traditionally connected with the Fourth of July.

FIVE

Those Lazy, Hazy Days of Summer
Celebrations of Love and Freedom

Asian folktales tell stories of summer lovers.

LONG AGO in the Heavens, there lived a cowherd and a weaver, who kept themselves busy serving the gods. One day, though, they met each other and fell in love. They were so entranced with each other that they forgot all about their work. All they wanted to do was spend time together.

Soon the gods were short of clothes and meat. When they realized that the two oblivious lovers had caused the shortages, the gods decided to separate them. They banished them to opposite sides of the heavenly river, the Milky Way.

The two lovers went back to work, but their hearts yearned for each other, and they wept as they toiled. At last the gods took pity on them; the two lovers would be allowed to reunite once a year, on July 7th.

Their reunion is called Tanabata, and some Japanese Americans still celebrate this day with paper decorations and fireworks. (In Japan, the holiday is an important time of festival.)

Chinese Americans also tell the story of the weaving maid and the cowherd. Their story varies somewhat from the Japanese version (for instance, the Weaving Girl is the daughter of the Emperor of Heaven, who is angry that his daughter would lower herself to become the wife of a humble cowherd), but both stories tell of love's fulfillment. In the Chinese story, on the seventh day of the seventh month, all the magpies of the world build a bridge across the heavenly river that separates the lovers—and the couple cross over to each other to spend one day together.

European summer traditions are a bit different. The midsummer solstice comes six months after Christmas, a dividing point on the year's circle of months. For centuries, people in Europe celebrated this day as Midsummer's Eve. European immigrants brought to the New World Midsummer bonfire-leaping traditions, since this was the day when the sun crossed the midpoint of the solar year. Swedish immigrants sometimes celebrated with a decorated Midsummer Tree. European folk traditions, like those rooted in Asia, considered this a time for lovers to be united.

Back in Europe, in the Middle Ages, the Catholic Church had renamed this festival St. John's Day, in an effort to "Christianize" a pagan festival. John the Baptist was the forerunner of Jesus who baptized Him in the river Jordan; Jesus once called him, "a burning and shining light," and so the Church tried to say that the midsummer fires should represent John instead of the sun. The metaphor was a bit strained, though, and it never caught on with the success of its opposite on the calendar, Christmas.

In the Old World, Swedish, German, and Welsh people once danced around maypoles on June 23; the poles were called Midsummer Trees or Midsummer Birches. In Wales, the branches of the tree were cut and used to decorate the pole, while bright streamers were used on Swedish and German maypoles. The dancing began at noon on Midsummer Eve, and in ancient times, it continued for nine days.

In the British Isles, the spirits of those who would die within the year were thought to walk abroad on Midsummer Eve. Many people

> According to the traditions of Britain and Northern Europe, fairies roam the earth on Midsummer's Eve. Shakespeare's play, *A Midsummer Night's Dream*, described a magical encounter between humans and the king and queen of fairies.

> Across North America, the period from late June to early July is still a time for lovers to be united, since these are the weeks when the most weddings take place.

would stay awake all night to prevent their souls from wandering. This was also a night for unmarried women to keep watch, hoping to be visited by the spirits of their future husbands.

Americans, however, created their own summer holiday—the Fourth of July, the celebration of America's independence from England. This holiday today is a time for picnics and fireworks, a time to relax and enjoy summer's warm weather.

Some African American communities celebrate July 5th as Emancipation Day—and even more observe Juneteenth (June 19th). Juneteenth is a growing holiday that celebrates the day in

> Every summer the Natchez people in the southern United States held a first fruits ceremony in early summer. No one was allowed to touch the ripe ears of corn in his own field until the ceremony was finished. In a similar ceremony, the Hopi of Arizona celebrated summer with masked dancers wearing bright paint and feathers. They represented the dancing spirits of rain and fertility called Kachinas, messengers between humans and the gods. At midsummer the Kachinas leave the Hopi villages to return to their homes in the mountains. While they are there, for half the year, they are believed to visit the dead underground.

This 19th-century Fourth of July card indicates that the patriotic holiday was also a time for lovers' meetings.

1865 when the Union soldiers, led by Major General Gordon Granger, landed at Galveston, Texas, with news that the war had ended and all slaves were now free (two and a half years after President Lincoln's Emancipation Proclamation). This holiday, like the Fourth of July, celebrates freedom with parades, barbeques, and baseball.

These summer celebrations grew from many different folk traditions—but they all mark the beginning of the summer season. They are times for feasting and fun, for romance and weddings, fireworks and outdoor celebrations. They honor both freedom and love—and they carry the message that life is good.

> According to some early American traditions, the Fourth of July was also a time for pranks. People would steal outhouses and front steps; wagons would be lifted into trees. Gradually, however, the custom of pranking shifted from the summer holiday to Halloween.

Fireworks brighten Fourth of July celebrations.

Fall holidays are apt to be spooky celebrations that flirt with death's shadows.

SIX

Glimpses of Another World
Halloween and Other
Celebrations of the Supernatural

Today Halloween is mostly a children's holiday when kids enjoy trick-or-treating in costumes.

WHEN EUROPEANS settled the New World, they brought with them many ancient traditions from the pre-Christians world. Some of these were still actively observed; others were like faint, persistent echoes that continued to live, half-hidden behind religious customs. The festival of Samhain was one of these long-ago echoes that lingered in the minds of European immigrants.

Samhain falls at the end of October (or the beginning of November), and the word meant the end of summer. Originally it was a farmers' festival that marked the time when crops were gathered and livestock was brought in from the pastures. Now the dark season of the year would begin, the time of short days and winter cold. In the folklore of Europe, the festival became associated with gloom, with death and the otherworld.

For the ancient **Celts**, this was the most important date in their calendar. They saw it as a boundary point between summer and winter, an in-between time outside of normal life. The day was said to create a crack between two realities, our ordinary everyday world and a world beyond. Supernatural creatures might easily slip through this crack, and so it was a dangerous night when the safety barriers between the worlds were no longer in place. People left out food for the wandering spirits, hoping to appease them. Irish folktales tell of strange encounters between mortals and fairyfolk at this time of the year. The dead were also said to walk the earth, and many claimed to catch glimpses of departed loved ones.

Irish immigrants to North America carried these stories with them. This fall festival was a time for gathering together and feasting, a time for remembering one's ancestors who had departed this life. Chairs were sometimes placed in front of the fire and food left waiting on the hearth for the dead to enjoy when they visited the household.

Back in the ninth century, however, the Catholic Church had tried to turn Samhain into a Christian holiday. October 31st became All Hallow's Eve; November 1st was transformed into All Saint's Day; and November 2nd was All Soul's Day. The Church wanted to **sanctify** these days of mystery and darkness as holy days of prayer for those who have died.

Today, few North Americans see All Hallow's Eve—Halloween—as a holy day. Instead, it is a time for pranks and spooky fun, for costumes and delicious shivers. Children dress up as Samhain's ghosts and goblins—and people give them candy and treats to ward off "tricks." For many North Americans, it is a day for mocking death by turning skeletons and demons into children's figures.

For Mexican Americans, the Day of the Dead (November 2nd) is public celebration with deeply per-

According to a 17th-century almanac:

At Hallowtide, slaughter time entereth in, And then doth the husbandman's feasting begin.

Fairies were thought to ride at Halloween, stealing men, women, and children. One woman named Isabel Gowdie claimed she was taken by the fairies "under the hills" where she met "the broad faced man who was king of the fairies . . . and the woman in white who was their queen." Today's claims of alien abductions echo these long-ago accounts of fairies.

sonal meaning. Schools and communities celebrate with art exhibits, fairs, and night processions—and meanwhile, families remember their dead. Cemeteries are cleaned and weeded, the gravestones scrubbed, and fresh flowers and candles are arranged on the graves.

Native Americans in the southwestern regions of North America believed that the soul of a dead person visits its relatives once a year—and the family must get ready for the visit by preparing the person's favorite food and drink, an offering to the soul.

According to tradition, witches, demons, and other nasty creatures wander the earth at Halloween.

JACK-O'-LANTERNS

According to an old folktale, a blacksmith named Jack was too evil to get into heaven . . . but he outwitted the devil and escaped hell. As he turned to go, he scooped up some glowing coals from hell's fires with the vegetable he was eating. With his lantern of devilish fire, he lights his way to wander the earth.

Jack O'Lantern was related to Will o' the Wisp, who snatched some burning straw from hell when he was turned away.

GUY FAWKES DAY

In 1605, a Catholic rebel named Guy Fawkes planned to blow up the Protestant House of Parliament; his plot was discovered, and he was executed on November 5th. A folk festival arose out of his story, and on Guy Fawkes Day, children built dummies out of straw and burned them.

This tradition was brought to the colonies, and it continues in Newfoundland as Bonfire Day. In New York City, Election Day bonfires are burned around the same time of year, continuing the custom even though the original reason behind it has been forgotten. But the fires of Samhain may lie deeper yet at the root of the original Guy Fawkes Day.

Glimpses of Another World

Day of the Dead figures poke fun at death.

    Mexican Americans combined these traditions with European customs. On the Day of the Day they continue to build *ofrendas*, altars where they leave offerings to show the dead they are still remembered and loved. These altars are decorated with flowers, fruit and other foods, cut tissue paper, photographs, and personal items that once belonged to the departed.

    To an even greater extent than the traditional Halloween celebrations, Day of the Dead festivities mock death. Candy, banners,

> Mexican Americans call marigolds the "flower of the dead" and they use them to decorate for Day of the Dead celebrations. These flowers are also used to form paths to guide the smallest dead back home.
>
> These small dead souls are the departed children of Mexican families. Candies, milk, sweet tamales, and the traditional *pan de muerto* (bread of the dead) will be placed on altars for these *angelitos* (little angels). The *angelitos* are thought to return on October 30 or 31, before the other dead. The families welcome the dead children with toys and other gifts. The *angelitos* then leave before the arrival of the other dead, who may be noisier and more dangerous.

and papier-maché figures all portray skulls and skeletons. Like Halloween, this is not a frightening day, but a day of laughter and fun.

Unlike Halloween, however, Day of the Dead celebrations hold a deeper dimension. According to this tradition, death is neither something to be feared and dreaded, nor something that can ultimately separate us from those we love. The dead and the living continue to interact, and both participate in the day's family reunions. The Day of the Dead celebrates the ultimate unity between the world of the dead and the world of the living.

Just as all folk festivals evolve and change over the years, the ancient holiday of Samhain was transformed into new shapes as it encountered first Christianity and then the New World. Today's celebrations look very different from the long-ago harvest feasts that marked the end of summer. Our modern world is far in time and space from the one that shaped Samhain's roots.

And yet despite the differences, we still hear that same echo,

> On the Day of the Dead, Mexican Americans light a candle for each soul to guide it home. The cemetery glows with the flames of hundreds of candles. Late into the evening women pray for the dead, while the men sing and drink.

lingering in the voices of trick-or-treaters, whispering from the bony grins of Day of the Dead skeletons. This is a time when we remember death. We may react with shivers and goose bumps; we may be filled with sadness as we think of those who are no longer with us, or the reminder may turn us to prayer. But despite this holiday's dark macabre side, despite the fear and sadness and solemn thoughts, this celebration in all its shapes and forms is still a joyous one. It affirms that in the end, life is stronger than death.

As is true with so many folk celebrations, light and fire play an important part in Halloween traditions. These candles may glimmer eerily from jack-o'-lantern faces, but they still light the darkness, symbolizing the power of life over death.

Harvest is a time of victory and achievement.

SEVEN

Harvest Home
Feasts of Gratitude

According to folk traditions, a boggart might threaten the fall harvest.

L̲ONG AGO IN ENGLAND, a farmer bought a patch of rich fertile land. He walked around his new property, well satisfied with his purchase, wondering what crop he would plant first. Suddenly, however, a **boggart** leaped out of nowhere, waving his long hairy arms.

"You're on my land!" the boggart yelled.

"I just bought it," the farmer replied. "It's mine."

"No, it isn't," screeched the boggart. "It's mine! It's mine!" He stamped his huge hairy feet.

The farmer didn't want to anger the ugly creature—but he didn't want to lose the rich crops he was planning either. "Let's strike a bargain," he said.

The boggart grinned, his teeth showing wide and yellow between his hairy lips. "Agreed! You do the work and we'll share the crops."

"Fine," said the farmer. "Do you want tops or bottoms?"

"Tops," said the boggart.

The boggart thought he had gotten the better of the farmer. But the crafty farmer fooled him by planting potatoes in the field. When harvest time came, the boggart got nothing but the stems and leaves. The boggart was determined to keep that from happening again, so the next year he asked for bottoms.

But this year the farmer planted barley. He got the grain, while the boggart was left with only the stubble and roots. The boggart scowled and growled, "This year you'll sow wheat. When it's ripe, we'll each harvest our own share."

The farmer was worried at first, but then he had an idea. He scattered iron rods through the boggart's side of the wheatfield. When the boggart arrived, he kept blunting his scythe on what he thought were the toughest weeds he'd ever seen.

The boggart finally flung down his dull scythe and screamed, "Keep this useless land!" He jumped in the air and came down with such a thud that a hole opened in the earth beneath him. He vanished into it and never bothered the farmer again.

But sometimes, at harvest time, tools go missing from farms. When that happens, peo-

---

Many ancient Harvest Home celebrations in the Old World included Corn Mother customs. The Corn Mother's spirit was said to possess the last sheaf of wheat left standing in the field—and the man who cut it became the Lord of the Harvest. These traditions were rooted in ancient Greek fertility rites that centered on Ceres, the goddess of the earth.

THE HISTORY OF THANKSGIVING

After that first celebration, the Pilgrims did not hold Thanksgiving the next year, or any year thereafter, though some of their descendants later celebrated a "Forefather's Day" that usually occurred on December 21 or 22. Several presidents, including George Washington, ordered one-time Thanksgiving holidays that occurred at various times of the year. In 1827, Mrs. Sarah Josepha Hale began lobbying for Thanksgiving as a national holiday, but her efforts were unsuccessful until 1863, when Abraham Lincoln finally made it a national holiday.

In Canada, Thanksgiving is celebrated on the second Monday of October.

The Pilgrims (pictured here on their way to church) built a community that centered on their religion.

ple shake their heads and roll their eyes. They know the boggart is up to his tricks.

In England and other European countries, harvest was an important time in the earth's cycle. Although most farmers did not match wits with a wily boggart, they did do constant battle with the capricious earth. Droughts and storms could all too easily destroy the food that was so desperately needed for the cold months ahead.

Native Americans play an essential role in Thanksgiving folklore.

When the harvest was successfully completed, it marked the end of months of hard work. It was a time of satisfaction and triumph, a time to celebrate.

When the Puritan settlers arrived in what is now the state of Massachusetts, they brought with them the Harvest Home traditions they had known back in the British Isles. They had good reason to celebrate: they had survived their first terrible months in the New World, and they were free to worship God as they wanted. The Plymouth colony was deeply religious, however, and so, after the first successful harvest, the colonists wanted more than just a celebration; they wanted a feast of thanksgiving to God.

According to legend, the Pilgrims ate the foods that Native Americans had shown them—turkey, pumpkins, corn, sweet potatoes, and cranberries. The Pilgrims invited their Indian friends to take part in their feast, and a new North American holiday was born—Thanksgiving.

The Pilgrims, the Native Americans, and their foods now have a permanent place in American folklore. Thanksgiving adds a new element to the old Harvest Home traditions, for the cele-

---

For the Iroquois people of the Northeast, thanksgiving was a year-round event, an essential part of each festival. This Thanksgiving Speech was used at every ceremony:

This is what He-Fashioned-Our-Lives did: He decided, "The only thing required of those moving about the earth is that they express their gratitude." That is the obligation of those of us gathered here: that we continue to be grateful. . . . The first thing for us to do is to be thankful for each other. . . .

Next, He-Fashioned-Our-Lives said, "I shall establish the earth. The people who move about will be in a relationship when they refer to the earth. They will say, 'Our mother who supports our feet.'" And it is true: we are using the earth every day and every night . . . we are obtaining from the earth the things that bring us happiness. Give it your thoughts, that we may give thanks properly. . . .

Then the Creator said, "The people will have love; they will simply be thankful. They will begin on the earth, giving thanks for all they see. They will carry it upward, ending where I dwell. . . .

PUMPKIN CAKE FOR SUKKOT

2 cups sugar
1¼ cup vegetable oil
1½ cups pumpkin puree (canned or fresh)
4 eggs
3 cups flour
2 tsp baking powder
2 tsp baking soda
2 tsp cinnamon
1 tsp salt
¾ cup seedless raisins
¾ cup golden raisins
1 cup chopped walnuts or pecans

Preheat oven to 350 degrees. Place sugar, oil, and pumpkin in large mixing bowl and beat well at medium speed. Add eggs one at a time. Mix well. Sift flour, baking soda and baking powder, cinnamon, and salt. Fold into batter. Stir in raisins and nuts. Pour into a 10-inch greased and floured tube pan or bundt pan. Bake 1¼ hours or until done. Test with a toothpick. Cool on rack before removing from pan.

> The Hebrew word *Sukkot* means "booths," and refers to the temporary dwellings Jews live in when they celebrate this holiday. The name of the holiday is frequently translated "the Feast of Tabernacles."

bration connects people not only to the earth but to each other, and to the Creator as well.

The Pilgrims transformed the traditions with which they were familiar by mixing them with ancient customs from the Jewish Scriptures (the Christians' Old Testament). Their thanksgiving celebration had something in common with the Jewish holiday of Sukkot.

Sukkot has a double meaning, one that's both historical and agricultural. The holiday commemorates the 40-year period during which the children of Israel were wandering in the desert, living in temporary shelters—and Sukkot is also a harvest festival. It is sometimes referred to as the Festival of Ingathering. In northeastern North America, Jews who celebrate this holiday build temporary shelters or huts. They often decorate these with dried squash and

> In the Hebrew Scriptures, this command was given to the Jews:
>
> *Celebrate the Feast of Tabernacles for seven days after you have gathered the produce of your threshing floor and your winepress. Be joyful at your Feast—you, your sons and daughters, your menservants and maidservants, and the Levites, the aliens, the fatherless and the widows who live in your towns. For seven days celebrate the Feast to the Lord your God. . . . For the Lord your God will bless you in all your harvest and all the work of your hands, and your joy will be complete.* (Deuteronomy 16:13–15)

PUMPKIN PIE

No Thanksgiving is complete without pumpkin pie. Here's a simple recipe you might want to try for your family's next fall celebration.

4 cups fresh pumpkin, cooked and mashed (Halloween jack-o'-lanterns can be cut up, frozen, and later cooked for your pie)
one 14-oz can of sweetened condensed milk
2 eggs
1 tsp cinnamon
½ tsp ginger
½ tsp nutmeg
½ tsp salt
one 9-inch pie crust (you can buy one already prepared)

Preheat oven to 425 degrees Fahrenheit. In a large bowl, combine the first 6 ingredients. When thoroughly blended, pour into pie crust. Bake for 15 minutes; then reduce heat to 350 degrees and bake another 35–40 minutes (until a knife inserted in the middle comes out clean).

corn, familiar decorations for Thanksgiving as well. Although the holiday falls earlier in the year than Thanksgiving (usually in September or October), the two holidays have much of the same flavors.

Both holidays are more than harvest festivals. They are ways to reenact the past, so that we never forget our roots. At the same time, both Thanksgiving and Sukkot are times to draw close to family and friends, to share special foods. Most of all, they are occasions to celebrate our gratitude for all we have been given.

Scottish North Americans connect to both their community and their past.

EIGHT

A Three-Strand Spiral
Celebrating the Past, the Community, and the Spiritual World

Unconsciously or consciously, many modern North Americans think of time as an arrow. Although older concepts of time may seem silly today, they may help us better understand the nature of time, since the arrow metaphor is not a perfect symbol for time's many qualities. (After all, if time is an arrow, who is shooting the arrow?)

If MOST OF US were to draw a picture of time, we would draw an arrow or a river—something linear that flows endlessly forward through space, carrying us all along with it. Ahead of us lies the future, behind us the past, but our only reality is our momentary present position in time's river.

Since Albert Einstein's work in the early 20th century, however, astronomers and physicists have begun to look at time in new ways. Time is no longer seen as an absolute and measurable quality. Instead, it is relative, depending on your perspective. Some scientists see it as a fourth dimension; others question the very nature of time or if it even exists at all.

Whatever time may or may not be at its deepest levels, everyday existence depends on keeping track of it in some way, so that we can manage the circumstances of our lives, practically, emotionally, spiritually. The older image of time as a circle is in some ways a more legitimate mental scheme for doing this.

When we think of time as an arrow or a river, we often fall into a love-hate relationship with time. On the one hand, we are always waiting for the good things the future will bring—but on the other hand, time seems to be constantly slipping away from us. We dread letting go of things, allowing them to fall into the past where they seem to disappear from reality. Time constantly wears away our lives.

When we want to save a moment of time, we sometimes snap a photograph, freezing the visual aspect of that moment forever. Telling stories is another way to put our experiences into a time capsule, something that can be saved and returned to whenever we want. And holiday rituals are a way to capture the past by reenacting it again and again.

Our deep-rooted folk celebrations offer us a way of thinking that treasures each point on time's cycle. Past, present, and future are all equally real and valuable. From this perspective the past never ceases to exist; it remains an important part of our identities both today and in the future.

However, as we travel time's cycles, we never return to exactly the same place. For example, Christmas comes each year, over and over and over. The cycle's repetitions seem changeless—and yet we are not unchanged; each Christmas does not find us the same. Every time December 25th rolls around yet again, we are a year older; different things interest us; new people may have joined our group of family and friends; and others may have left. Time by its very nature brings change.

That's why some thinkers have suggested that time's cycles should be compared to a spiral. We move around an endless circle, from season to season, marking our journey with celebrations and holidays. With each revolution of the cycle, we find ourselves back where we started—but at a different point on the spiral. We look at the same holiday event from a slightly altered perspective.

As we find our place in time's spiral, we also find our identity. We might think of this process as having three strands. One is the line

---

Have you ever noticed that time seems to flow faster now than when you were younger? When you were five, the months between each Christmas or from one birthday to the next may have seemed like a lifetime—but as you grow older, you may notice that the year's wheel seems to spin faster.

Some researchers now believe that there is a chemical reason for this phenomenon. As we grow older, they say, the **dopamine** levels in our brain change, altering the way we perceive the passage of time.

running from the past through the present to the future; the second is the bond that connects us to one another; and the third is the invisible tie we may feel to a realm that reaches beyond time. Holidays and festivals act as time's markers—and they braid together these three strands of our identity. The special days we celebrate each year tie us to the past; they link us with each other; and they connect us in some way to something deeper.

For instance, Jews in North America and around the world

The Seder foods all have special meanings:

- Haroseth is a mixture of chopped walnuts, wine, cinnamon, and apples that represents the mortar the Jewish slaves used to assemble the Egyptian Pharaoh's bricks.
- Parsley symbolizes springtime: it is dipped in salt water to remind the celebrants of the Jewish slaves' tears.
- Roasted egg is another symbol of spring.
- A shank bone stands for the sacrificial lamb offering; the bone can come from whatever the family is eating, such as the leg bone of a roasted turkey.
- Bitter herbs are freshly grated horseradish that reflect the bitter affliction of slavery.

Passover celebrations give ongoing life to ancient Hebrew Scriptures.

> During the Seder four glasses of wine are poured to represent the stages of the Exodus
>
> 1. freedom
> 2. deliverance
> 3. redemption
> 4. release
>
> A fifth cup of wine is called the Cup of Elijah, an offering for the Prophet Elijah. During the Seder the door to the home is opened to invite the prophet Elijah in.

relive a defining moment in their past whenever they celebrate a Seder meal as part of Passover. By reenacting the experience of their ancestors, they bring the story of the **Exodus** into the present, where each generation can experience it for themselves. With each Passover celebration, Jews affirm their link to a community that reaches far into the past, and at the same time they express anew their faith. They draw their sense of identity from these connections to the past, the community, and God.

As we spiral through time, however, festivals like these evolve and grow. Passover's time-honored celebrations are not frozen and static slices of time. Like all living traditions, new dimensions of meaning are constantly being attached to the older symbols. The same ceremony may express different ideas and values (or at least express these values in a different

> Jewish Americans seeking to honor women's role in their religion fill Miriam's Cup with water, symbolizing the miracle of Miriam's well that sustained the Israelites during their long desert journey to the Promised Land.

language) to different generations. For example, as women's importance is increasingly recognized in North American society, some Jews have adopted new Seder rituals to honor the role of Miriam, Moses' sister and the Prophetess in the Exodus. By adding a second cup, called Miriam's Cup, to the Passover dinner table along with Elijah's Cup, modern-day Jews highlight the past and present contributions of women to Jewish culture. Because it can be adapted to modern needs, the ancient tradition still lives and breathes.

In a similar way, Vietnamese immigrants to North America continue to celebrate Tet, Vietnamese New Year, just as generations of Vietnamese people have done before them. In a new land, far from the home of their ancestors, they remain firmly tied to their past even as they adapt to the present. The holiday helps them build a deep sense of community and it affirms their spiritual beliefs.

In 1980, in a suburb of Washington, D.C., Vietnamese immigrants offered this prayer on Tet:

> According the Hebrew book of Exodus (12:14), after God delivered the Jews from their Egyptian captors, he told them:
>
> "This is a day you are to commemorate; for the generations to come you shall celebrate it as a festival to the Lord—a lasting ordinance."

We bow down our heads in front of the altar of our Ancestors and respectfully set up these few offerings of tea and fruit.
We set up an incense stick and put in it our piety.
Our hearts in pain as we remember the Old Country.
Our souls . . . dreaming like butterflies.
Our eyes filled with tears as we remember all that is far away.
We pledge to keep our roots and morality in wait of that day.

> Vietnamese Americans wear red for Tet to symbolize their happiness.

> *We pledge to maintain our courage and follow our ancestors, so as to maintain our millennium-old culture at all cost, so as to keep our essence as Vietnamese.*
>
> *We therefore make these pure if modest offerings, and bow to you a thousand times, a hundred times, asking that you bless our land and grant it Peace.*
>
> *Please accept our prayers.*

Clearly, the Tet holiday continued to meet the needs of these Vietnamese Americans far from their homeland. It gave them present strength to endure past hardships with hope for the future. In a new land, in new circumstances, the ancient celebration was flexible enough to take on new meaning as it shaped the community's ongoing identity.

St. Patrick's Day is another holiday that has adapted to the present in order to tie the community to the past, to each other, and to their faith. In Ireland, the holiday was a day of prayer, a time to go to church and think quiet thoughts. In North America, however, the day has been transformed into an often rowdy celebration of Irish-American heritage. The "wearin' of the green" affirms the Irish community's identity; it ties them to their shared heritage, a heritage that includes faith in God . . . and a playful sense of magic and possibility. After all, the Irish shamrock brings good luck to whoever wears it—and the leprechaun's pot of gold may lie at the foot of any rainbow.

Holidays like these bind us together. You may be furious with your brother—but as you join the family around the Christmas tree, you forget your differences. Aunt Trudy may not be your favorite relative—but you still sit down with her at Thanksgiving dinner. And the kid next door may drive you crazy—but at Halloween you put candy in his bag and think how cute he looks in his costume. No matter what separates us, whether time or space

Festivals mark our place in time—but they also interrupt ordinary time in one or more ways:

- with rituals of purification (like Lent or Yom Kippur).
- with rites of passage (like graduation and bar mitzvah celebrations).
- with rites of reversal (like Mardi Gras, when people behave in ways they wouldn't normally).
- with rites of conspicuous display (like the parades of Memorial Day).
- with rites of conspicuous consumption (like Thanksgiving).
- with ritual dramas (like the Passover Seder ceremonies).
- with rites of exchange (like Christmas).
- with rites of competition (like the Superbowl or the Kentucky Derby).

Knotwork like this design graphically symbolizes the Celtic belief that life is an interwoven pattern. The past, the community, and the spiritual world are ongoing realities that weave through the four seasons' celebrations.

A Three-Strand Spiral

This 19th-century illustration shows the "wearin' of the green," a tradition that celebrates North America's Irish heritage.

or negative emotions, these celebrations draw us back together. They nourish our roots—and they give meaning to our future.

According to ancient Celtic traditions, the earth's turning points—the major festivals of winter, spring, summer, and fall—are "thin" times, times when the walls we keep around our ordinary lives become transparent and weak. Memories of the past, our bonds to each other, and the spiritual realm all become tangible at each holiday celebration. Remembering where we came from, who we are, and what we believe, we are strengthened for our spiral journey on through time.

Community parades offer a time to connect with each other and our shared past.

A Three-Strand Spiral

WINDOWS INTO A COMMUNITY

All over North America, around the year's entire circle, festivals take place, celebrating some aspect of a particular community's life. If you look at the list of festivals below, you can catch a glimpse of what's important to the people of that region.

January
Ice Fishing Derby: Antioch, Illinois
Winter Carnival: Quebec City, Quebec
Basque Festival: Boise, Idaho

February
Rattlesnake Roundup: Opp, Alabama
Island Shrimp Festival: Ft. Meyers, Florida
Cherry Blossom Festival: Honolulu, Hawaii

March
Maple Sugar Festival: Monterey, Virginia
Curling Days: Cobourg, Ontario
Chalo Nitka Tribe Festival: Moore Haven, Florida

April
Crayfish Festival: Breaux Bridge, Louisiana
Cotton Festival: McKinney, Texas
Winter Fair: Brandon, Manitoba

May
King Crab Festival: Kodiak, Alaska
Blessing of Animals: Santa Barbara, California
Pea Festival: Milton-Freewater, Oregon

June
Midnight Sun Baseball: Fairbanks, Alaska
Fiesta of Five Flags: Sarasota, Florida
Discovery Day: Newfoundland

July
Logger's Celebration: Priest River, Idaho
Strawberry Festival: Chatham, Massachusetts
Lumberjack Days: Bigfork, Minnesota

September
Grape Festival: Sonoma, California
Soybean Festival: La Plata, Missouri
Threshers' Reunion: Mt. Pleasant, Iowa

October
Turkey Calling Contest: Yellville, Arkansas
Chrysanthemum Festival: Bristol, Connecticut
Apple Festival: Jackson, Ohio

November
Speckled Trout Rodeo: Gulf Shores, Alabama
Blessing the Hounds: Lexington, Kentucky
Swamp Buggy Days: Naples, Florida

December
Winter Night Koshare Ceremonies: La Junta, Colorado
Our Lady of Guadalupe Procession: Taos, New Mexico
St. Lucia Festival: Rockford, Illinois

Further Reading

Bonnice, Sherry. *Christmas and Santa Claus Folklore*. Philadelphia: Mason Crest, 2003.

Carey, Diana and Judy Large. *Festivals, Family and Food*. Stroud, U.K.: Hawthorne Press, 1996.

Druitt, Ann, Christine Fynes-Clinton, and Marjie Rowling. *All Year Round*. New York: Gryphon House, 1997.

Fitzjohn, Sue, Minda Weston, and Judy Large. *Festivals Together: A Guide to Multicultural Celebration*. Stroud, U.K.: Hawthorne Press, 1993.

McCaffrey, Kerri. *Masking and Madness: Mardi Gras in New Orleans*. New York: Viss d'Arte Books, 2001.

Sanna, Ellyn. *Food Folklore*. Philadelphia: Mason Crest, 2003.

Santino, Jack. *All Around the Year*. Urbana: University of Illinois Press, 1994.

Schweid, Eleizer and Amnon Hardy. *The Jewish Experience of Time*. Northvale, N.J.: Jason Aronson, 2000.

Stokker, Kathleen. *Keeping Christmas: Yuletide Traditions in the New Land*. St. Paul: Minnesota Historical Society, 2000.

For More Information

Celebrating the World of Festivals and Events
www.festivals.com

Holidays on the Net
www.holidays.net

Holidays—USA
www.holidayfestival.com/USA.html

Jewish Holidays and Festivals
www.melizo.com

World Wide Holidays and Festivals
www.holidayfestival.com

Glossary

Boggart A mischievous creature from Britain; the word is the root for "bogeyman."
Carnival A festival of merrymaking before Lent.
Celts An early Indo-European people that spread from Asia Minor to Spain and Britain; they were the ancestors of today's Irish, Scotch, Welsh, and Bretons.
Communion The Christian ritual that reenacts Christ's Last Supper before his death.
Dopamine A chemical that passes messages between brain cells.
Effigy A three-dimensional image used to represent a person.
Equinox Either of the two times each year (March 21 and September 23) when the sun crosses the equator, and day and night are the same length everywhere.
Exodus The long-ago departure of the Jews from Egypt, recorded in the Hebrew Scriptures and reenacted at the Jewish holiday of Passover.
Immigrants People who leave their homeland to settle in another country.
Medieval Having to do with the Middle Ages, the period in Europe from about A.D. 500 to 1500.
Metaphors Symbols or figures of speech that often allow concrete objects to symbolize or help explain the meanings of more abstract concepts.
Nativity Birth (usually used in reference to the birth of Christ).
Pagan A person who believes in the old earth religions.
Sanctify Make holy.
Solstice The two times each year (June 22 and December 22) when the sun is farthest from the equator.
Wake A community time to visit the body of a dead person.

Index

African American celebrations 33, 34, 62
April Fool's Day 57
Asian American celebrations 50, 55, 57, 58, 61, 96–97

birthdays 18
boggart 79–81

Christmas 15, 20, 25, 26, 28, 31, 32, 35
Corn Mother 80

Day of the Dead 70–71, 73, 74, 75

earth's cycles 54, 98, 99
Easter 50, 53–54, 55

Feast of Tabernacles 85
food 18
Fourth of July 15, 60, 62, 63, 64, 65

Groundhog's Day 43
Guy Fawkes Day 72

Halloween 40, 64, 66, 68, 70, 71
Hanukkah 29–31
harvest 76, 80, 81–83, 85
Harvest Home traditions 80, 82, 83
Holi 49, 51, 57

Kwanzaa 33, 34

life over death 75
light 18, 27–28, 29-31, 32, 33, 55, 75
love 61–62, 63

Mardi Gras 50–51, 52, 53
Midsummer's Eve 62

Native American celebrations 10, 33, 41, 46, 48, 49, 63, 71, 82, 83
new life 44, 47–48, 54, 55, 57
New Year's Day 28
numbers 17

Passover 55, 94, 95, 96
past 92, 95, 97, 100

resurrection 5
rituals 15

Samhain 69–70, 74
Seder 93, 95, 96
St. Patrick's Day 97, 99
Sukkot 84, 85, 87

Thanksgiving 80, 82, 83, 85, 87
time 8, 9–10

Valentine's Day 36, 38, 39, 40–41, 42, 43

winter solstice 26

Biographies

Ellyn Sanna has authored more than 50 books, including adult nonfiction, novels, young adult biographies, and gift books. She also works as a freelance editor and helps care for three children, a cat, a rabbit, a one-eyed hamster, two turtles, and a hermit crab.

Dr. Alan Jabbour is a folklorist who served as the founding director of the American Folklife Center at the Library of Congress from 1976 to 1999. Previously, he began the grant-giving program in folk arts at the National Endowment for the Arts (1974–76). A native of Jacksonville, Florida, he was trained at the University of Miami (B.A.) and Duke University (M.A., Ph.D.). A violinist from childhood on, he documented oldtime fiddling in the Upper South in the 1960s and 1970s. A specialist in instrumental folk music, he is known as a fiddler himself, an art he acquired directly from elderly fiddlers in North Carolina, Virginia, and West Virginia. He has taught folklore and folk music at UCLA and the University of Maryland and has published widely in the field.